Dear Rickey,
    My story is only a story
of the chance in life which
America brings to all Boys
and Girls.
    I send you a book.
        Yours faithfully,
            Herbert Hoover

HERBERT HOOVER

The Waldorf Astoria Towers
New York, New York

Dear Rickey:

        My story is only a story of the
chance in life which America brings to
all boys and girls.

        I send you a book.

        Yours faithfully,

            Herbert Hoover

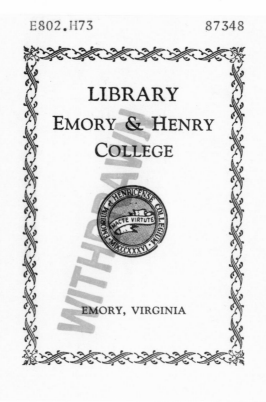

ON GROWING UP

On Growing Up

LETTERS TO AMERICAN BOYS & GIRLS

INCLUDING "THE UNCOMMON MAN"

AND OTHER SELECTIONS

BY HERBERT HOOVER

EDITED BY WILLIAM NICHOLS

WILLIAM MORROW & COMPANY · *New York* 1962

Second Printing, October 1962

To
the Boys and Girls
of
America

FOREWORD

As THE ELDERS used to say: "I am moved to speak my mind." This time, in defense of our present crop of children.

If we appraise them as they appear in the press and in the abundant statistics of crime, we would believe that children of today are a bad example of this species.

I can claim some experience with children. I was a kid once. I grew up on sand-lot baseball, swimming holes, and fishing with worms. I had a minor part in raising two boys of my own. I directed the food supply to hundreds of millions of children, and I also directed the rehabilitation of tens of millions of them—the victims of famine and disease. And I have for twenty-five years had a hand in administering the Boys' Clubs which look after six hundred thousand boys. I have received these thousands of letters from children which prove their high aspirations when growing up.

From these experiences, I have developed some ideas of what goes on in children's minds. They are not born evil. They are endowed with a cheerfulness and a surplus of dynamic energy and a self-starter which demands exercise at any moment. They are bundles of affection. They are ambitious, joyous, and anxious to take part in the serious business of the world. They have more awareness of the world around them than had the kids of my generation. A child, being naturally and uninhibitedly

‹§ 9 §›

inquisitive, demands more information every half-hour. They are intent on discovering the world for themselves.

To prove all this, I offer this correspondence with children. In fairness to the youngsters, I have omitted all names and addresses. The master file of this correspondence is available to demonstrate that these children's letters are genuine and that I have no ghost writer.

Answering these letters, of which these are only specimens, has been a great relief from sleepless nights haunted by public anxieties, and they are a restoration of confidence in America's future.

Herbert Hoover

NEW YORK, JUNE, 1962

EDITOR'S PREFACE

THERE IS A STORY of the famous novelist who once told his publisher that he planned to write a book about child care. The publisher, a doubting man, immediately asked what the novelist's qualifications might be. To which the great novelist replied with quiet dignity:

"I am a former child."

Just so, in the pages that follow, you will find Herbert Hoover writing not as a former President, but as a former Boy. It is a role which suits him well. He has always loved the memory of his own boyhood, with a grave, affectionate, and wisely humorous regard for all boys and girls who are engaged in the serious business of growing up.

In the course of a long and honored career, that concern expressed itself in many ways, such as his labors to feed hundreds of millions of hungry children after two World Wars . . . his calling of the famous White House Conference on Child Health and Protection in November 1930 . . . or his leadership, for twenty-six years, in the great work of the Boys' Clubs of America.

But his concern expresses itself most eloquently, I believe, in his answers to letters like those which follow. They are chosen from the thousands of letters which, however spelled, somehow found their way each month to his home in the "Walled Off Hotel" in New York; and which, however busy, he somehow found time to answer with his own special mixture of wisdom and gaiety.

As editor there is little more for me to say—for, in editing, I have had so little to do. Except for the changes and emendations needed to protect the privacy of the youngsters, all of the letters appear as received; and the answers are as written, first in longhand by Mr. Hoover, and then transcribed by his secretary, Miss Bernice Miller, and the faithful members of "The Staff."

And this seems the place to thank Fred Farrar for his particular help in guiding the physical appearance of this book.

A few of the letters, and related selections, have appeared previously in the pages of *Reader's Digest*, or *This Week Magazine*. The extent and intensity of the response to these "samples" make me feel that many American boys and girls—and their parents—will find pleasure and inspiration in the pages which follow.

WILLIAM NICHOLS

CONTENTS

❀

CONTENTS

PART 1

On Boyhood Days

GOOD START

Dear Sir:

I am a Cub Scout. We are studying about Presidents. I would like some information about your boyhood or some interesting fact about your life.

                    Yours truly,
                    Ronnie ———

My dear Ronnie:

I have your letter, and am proud to be under examination by a Cub Scout.

I had a joyful boyhood on a farm and under the guardianship of a country doctor.

The most interesting fact about my life is that due to the kindness and care of those persons, I was given a tough body. I have lived for more than eighty-seven years.

I have worked in over fifty different nations of the world. When you get older, you will find books giving the details. In the meantime I am sending you part of a speech which I made about my own growing-up.*

* See page 147 of this book.

INTERROGATION POINT!

Dear Sir:

I am in fifth grade Sunday school class that is studing what it means to be christian. we are interested in knowing why you decided to go in to politics an how long did it take you to go through school? What age were you when you begain to think about the kind of work you would like to do? We wondered too when you first began to know about God and if you went to church as a little boy. My mother tolds me she belived you were a Quaker as you were a cousin of my grandfather. I know my grandfather went to church as a very smal boy.

Now you can began to see the second reason I am writing. Do you rember my grandfather? . . . . He is now 88 years old an is failing fast. He still gets around some but not like he did. The wenter months are hard on him.

Well I would like an answer to both parts of my letter but if you can't remember my grandfather do at least answer the first part.

Your frind
Onida ———

My dear Onida:

I think you are an interrogation point! But keep on asking questions all of your life.

As to your specific inquiries:

1. I did not originally "decide to go into politics." I was summoned to government service when the First World War broke out in 1914.

2. I was in school (including night school when an office boy) and college for sixteen years.

3. I was sixteen when I began to hope I might become an engineer.

4. I was taken to "Quaker Meeting" when I was a baby —there were no baby-sitters around.

5. I spent my first ten years at West Branch, Iowa. I do not remember many people there but that name sounds familiar.

6. I am sorry your Grandfather is ailing at eighty-eight years of age. I have the same number, but am still going strong.

IOWA DAYS

Dear Mr. Hoover:

I am studying famous people of Iowa in school and would like to know a little of your childlife in Iowa and other times you have spent in Iowa. I would be most grateful for any information or even a letter you would be able to send me.

Yours truly,
Susie ———

My dear Susie:

As a youngster in Iowa, my recollections are of the winter snows, sliding down hills on a homemade sled, trapping rabbits, searching the woods for nuts. Plus doing the household and farm chores. And growing strong on my aunt's good cooking.

HONESTY

Dear Mr. Hoover:

We at ———— High School believe that honesty is essential to the survival of our present civilization. Our Honor Creed, written by a former student, reads as follows: As a student of ————, I will strive to uphold the high standards of honesty, character, and personal integrity that are recognized as the ideal of a rich, full and useful life.

To encourage those who fall short of these standards we have an Honor Council, composed of ten students of unquestionable integrity that are recognized as leaders. These people talk confidentially to students who are known to be dishonest in any way. We have had many students tell us that such talks have helped them get on the right track.

Although being honest is an everyday job, we have an Honor Week each year, during which we place special emphasis on honesty in the form of posters, assembly program, and messages over the public address system. This year we want to let our students know "What others say about honesty." Because of your experience we feel that you have some very strong convictions about the value of being honest that influence many students. We would appreciate a message including such ideas to use as a part of our program for Honor Week.

Yours truly,
Jane ————

Dear Jane:

I wish all high schools were organized that way.

When I was a boy being taught writing in the first grade, I was required to copy various sentences at the top of a page in a ruled copy book. One of them made an impression which lasted for many years: "Honesty is the best policy."

It should read: "Honesty is imperative."

Therefore, I am for your system. It will make happier minds in school days and those days will come only once in your lives.

FIRST JOB

Dear Mr. Hoover:

Our ninth grade class is conducting an interview. We could write to anyone we please. I have chosen you.

Would you please answer these questions if possible.

1. What was your first job?
2. Of all the Presidents which one do you admire the most?
3. Can you speak anyother language besides English, if so which ones?
4. If you were in President Kennedy's place what would you do about the Berlin crisis?
5. What do you think of Premiere Khrushchevs actions?

Yours truly,
Dennis ———

My dear Dennis:

1: Household and farm chores were my first jobs. They were unpaid. My first regular paying job was office boy.

2: My greatest admiration is for both Washington and Lincoln, but we have also had other great Presidents.

3: I once spoke sufficient French to get around on railways and in hotels—but not enough to negotiate with governments.

4: I would do exactly what he is doing.

5: I have a very poor opinion of him in every respect.

WAS IT TRUE?

Dear Mr. Hoover:

I am your seventh cousin.

In a story I read, about Mr. Edison, you were riding on a train, and Mr. Edison was selling papers and candy, like he did when he was a little boy. Is this story true?

Very Truly Yours
Janice ———

My dear Seventh Cousin:

That story is true.

Mr. Henry Ford had given a great party for his old friend, Mr. Edison. The guests were brought from Detroit to Dearborn in an old-fashioned car and Mr. Edison sold peanuts as he did on that train when a boy.

Like the rest of us he liked to be a boy again.

WHO WAS YOUR IDOL?

Dear Mr. Hoover:

As an ardent admirer of yours, I beg a few moments of your valuable time. I am fifteen years old, and ever since I can remember, you have been my idol. When you were my age, did you also have an idol? If so who was he, and why was he your idol? If you would just answer this question, you will make me your servant forever. I wish you long life, good health, and happiness.

Most respectfully yours,
Lester ———

My dear Lester:

Yes—I had an idol. He was Abraham Lincoln.

WHAT WAS YOUR FAVORITE QUOTE?

Dear Mr. Hoover:

I am a student of history and am preparing a book of favorite quotes of famous people. I would appreciate it to have yours among the collection.

Sincerely,
Joyce-Ann ———

Dear Joyce-Ann:

My favorite quote is the Sermon on the Mount.

ADVICE

Dear Mr. Hoover:

Our 8th grade class would like to have you answer the question in the following paragraph.

How can young people of America help to keep peace in the world?

Sincerely,
David ———

Dear David:

As you say you are in the eighth grade, my advice is:

1. Work hard in school hours to get some indestructible things stored in your head.

2. Play every chance you get—including fishing.

3. Keep the rules of sport.

4. Don't begin to worry about international affairs until after you go to college. There is nothing you can do about them at this time of your life.

WHAT ARE YOU DOING NOW?

Dear Mr. Hoover:

I am an eighth grade student in Junior High School.

I would appreciate it so much and would consider it an honor if you could find the time to write me a personal letter—or have one of your secretaries do so—since I know you must be very busy—and tell me what you are *now* doing.

Thank you very much.

Yours sincerely,
Frank ———

Dear Frank:

My secretaries might use too much time and paper if they replied to your inquiry, so I will do it for you.

I am busy writing books on history. I believe in that old saying, "Those who do not remember the past are condemned to relive it."

Also, I am a chairman, director, or trustee in the administration of nine educational, scientific or charitable institutions.

No former President can, or should, cease from public service.

PART 2

On Being President

HOW TO BECOME PRESIDENT

Dear Mr. Hoover,

I am a boy 10 years old and who would like to become President like you were when I grow up. I thought that if I wrote to you that you can give me some information how you got to be a President. I wish you would send me an autograph. I would like that very much.

Your friend,
Martin ———

Dear Martin:

I am in favor of your ambition to be President. As to your request on the rules as to "how to get to be President," I suggest that:

The first rule is just to be a boy getting all the constructive joy out of life;

The second rule is that no one should win the Presidency without honesty and sportsmanship and consideration for others in his character—together with religious faith;

The third rule is that he should be a man of education.

If you follow these rules, you will be a man of standing in your community even if you do not make the White House. And who can tell? Maybe that also.

⋖ 35 ⋗

THE PRESIDENCY

Dear Sir:

Since you are such a busy person I will not burden you with a lot of questions. Among the questions I would like to ask—When you were in the eighth grade did you dream of being President, And what advice would you give the present teenager about being a future politician.

Sincerely yours,
Linda ———

My dear Linda:

I have your kind letter.

1. I did not "dream about becoming President" until forty-four years after I finished the eighth grade. I was busy on other things.

2. Being a politician is a poor profession. Being a public servant is a noble one. So my advice is to refocus your ambition.

CHANGING TIMES

Dear Mr. Hoover:

We are presently studying famous people. I thought I might ask you some questions.

When you were in office, was it very exciting? Did you travel much? What did you think of crime then? What do you think of it today?

What do you think of the world problems of today?

I hope to hear from you soon,

Sincerely yours,
Gordon ———

My dear Gordon:

Your questions just about stump me.

I abhor crime—always have and do so now. It is the greatest danger to America today.

Presidents must travel in order to learn what the people have in mind and to explain their policies.

However, travel has improved for Presidents. George Washington required five or six days to go with horses from New York to Washington. Presidents today can do it now in one hour by jet. But jets go over the heads of the people—like some of the speeches.

MONEY MATTERS

Dear Mr. Hoover:

Our Senior high school class has been studying problems concerning the running of our government. One of the items we have questioned has been the adequacy of the present salary for President.

We have decided to write to ex-presidents and ask them their opinion. Would you please answer these questions for us? We realize that much of this is of a personal nature, but we would appreciate any reflections that you can give us on this matter.

1. Is the Salary adequate at this time?

2. Was it necessary for you to use your own money during your tenure in office?

3. Is the pension for ex-presidents necessary? Should this be given immediately upon retirement from office, or should it be started at the customary retirement age of 65?

Thank you for your time and consideration in answering our questions.

Yours truly,
Neal ——

Dear Neal:

My answers to your questions are:
1. The President's salary is adequate.
2. I spent my own money in addition to my salary in order to meet what I believed were my obligations.
3. The pensions to former Presidents are not necessary to keep them alive. They can earn a living. However, the pensions and staff given to them enable the former Presidents to respond to demands upon them for continued public service.

PROBLEMS

Dear Sir:

I have heard and read much about you. I also know that you were the thirty-first president. Today the big problem is the Atom and Space; what was it when you were president? What did you enjoy most while being the president? What are your present interests?

Sincerely Yours,

Linda ———

My dear Linda:

My answers to your questions are:

1. I do not agree that the whole problem today concerns the atom bomb and space. Those are only parts of a larger problem—the determination of the Communists to rule the world.

2. The greatest problems during my administration were the Great Depression, our weak banking system, disarmament, an invasion of China by Japan, and many domestic reforms which were needed.

3. The thing I enjoyed most were visits from children. They did not want public offices. Also, I liked baseball and football games.

4. My present interests—at eighty-seven plus—are mostly writing books and occasionally going fishing.

SYMBOL

Dear Mr. Hoover:

I am a girl in the eighth grade who recently saw an article in a newspaper which expressed your feelings toward the office of the president. It read:

"I believe the presidentcy is more than an executive responsibility. It is the inspiring symbol of all that is highest in American purposes and ideals."

How do you think the job of our president has changed since you were our president, considering the conflicts we now have with the Congo, Russia and Berlin?

I have heard that you are a man experienced in world help. How do you feel the United States could best help the starving people of the world?

Sincerely yours,
Donna ———

My dear Donna:

I have your charming letter. As to your questions:

1. The responsibilities of the Presidency have not changed, the job has become greater as the Government employees, including the military forces, have grown from six hundred thousand to about five or six million.

2. The President's responsibilities to preserve peace have become much more difficult, as we have no peace from the last war.

3. I think America should use all her surplus food to save people from starving, irrespective of race, religion or form of Government, providing Americans can be appointed to distribute it. Otherwise, some of it would not reach the hungry people.

THE BURDEN

Dear President Hoover:

I am almost nine. I am in 3rd grade—Elementary School. I am in the first reading group.

I like History. Did you like being President. How are You?

Please wright. I now you busy.

Yours truly.

Joe ———

My dear Joe:

I am glad you like history.

As to your question, being President in time of unemployment and hardship is not too happy an experience.

WHAT WAS IT LIKE?

Dear Mr. Hoover:

Would you please tell me what it was like to carry the burdon of heading our great nation?

What was the United States like during your term?

Thank you very much and my highest regards to a great American.

> Respectfully yours,
> Jacque ———

Dear Jacque:

I am indeed obliged for your gracious expressions. As to your questions:

During my term the people were subjected to the great trial of a world-wide depression which swept over us from Europe. We adopted measures to prevent suffering and laid the foundations for recovery. That recovery came alongside the recovery of the rest of the world but was somewhat delayed by some foolish legislation. Nevertheless, the fundamental economic strength of America was victorious over both depression and the Second World War.

THE GREAT DEPRESSION

Dear Mr. Hoover:

I am a senior at High School, and am especially interested in American history. I would like to have your views on the Great Depression.

May God bless you.

Very cordially yours,
Gloria ———

Dear Gloria:

I have your letter inquiring about the Great Depression, and I am gratified for your kind expressions and your blessing. I am glad you are interested in depressions for they are an important part of our country's history.

Small depressions have arisen in American economy periodically over the years from excessive optimism and speculation.

The Great Depression came upon us when we were weakened by a collapse in speculation. At the same time there was an economic panic and collapse in Europe arising from the First World War. They were unable to purchase our products, and our prices—especially farm prices —collapsed. I do not see any economic collapse coming in Europe at the present time.

I hope you never see one of these great economic cyclones.

However, if you are interested you might borrow a book of mine entitled The Great Depression *from your library.*

SUPPORTER

Dear Mr. Hoover:

I am a thirteen year old girl in the eighth grade. Our civics teacher is having us write a term paper on different presidents of the United States. I have chosen you.

My parents and I are strong Republicans and we share an admiration of you and the multitude of outstanding things you have done in your life.

My mother is a history teacher, and she thinks your plan for meeting the problems of a depression was better, by far, than the program adopted by the Democrats.

I would appreciate a note from you to include with my report on your life.

Thank you.

Very truly yours,
Miss Jane ———

Dear Jane:

As a Republican I cannot fail to reply to another, especially to one who approves of my activities.

With all good wishes.

WOMEN PRESIDENTS

Dear President Hoover:

My Dad thinks you are the smartest living president, so I would like to have your opinion on this question: What are the chances of there ever being a woman president of the United States?

Best wishes to you,

Sincerely,
Kathy ———

My dear Kathy:

As a generalization, the men have not done too good a job of government in the world in the last forty-seven years, and the chances for the women are thereby increased.

With good wishes to you if you are a candidate for President about thirty years hence.

EX-PRESIDENTS

Dear Mr. Hoover:

I am a high school senior studying American government. For my term paper I am writing on the question of whether or not ex-presidents should be given a seat-at-large in the U.S. Senate.

Sincerely,
Lenore ———

My dear Lenore:

I have, in days gone by, advocated that very thing, but without a vote. However, at eighty-seven plus I would not be interested in sitting on a hard-bottom chair all day listening to other people's speeches.

SECOND GUESS

Dear Sir:

What kind of a situation do you think we would be in if you were president now!

Yours truly,
Robert ———

Dear Robert:

I am eighty-seven years plus; somebody much younger should be President now. Therefore, I do not lie awake speculating on this subject. But I am glad you are thinking about it.

SUMMING UP

Dear Mr. Hoover:

I am in the eighth grade. I would like to know when and why you became interested in politics, what offices you have held and when you held them. What were your likes and dislikes about politics? What are they now? If you had your life to live over again, would you live it the way you have or what changes would you make?

Yours truly,
Rickey ———

Dear Rickey:

It is generally held that I was not a good "politician." So my advice in that quarter is not worth much.

My life was made by my surroundings in good families, in school and in college. After that, it was made by the circumstances I was called upon to meet.

I don't know that I could do it any better if I had to do it over again, unless the world in which I lived from day to day had been different. In any event, the world has been very kind to me most of the time.

GOOD LUCK!

Dear Mr. Hoover:

You'r my favorite President of all 35! Remember the year of '32? and most of all 1928. It sure must have been hard getting the United States togeather during the depression! Golly you actually saw Wilson, Harding & Coolidge. Gee! What can a boy say to a President.

Well lots of luck and years ahead.

John ———

Dear John:

A boy does not need to say any more than you have to warm one's heart.

R.S.V.P.

Dear Mr. Hoover:

How does it feel to be a former president. What is your hobby? When is your birthday? Is it hot in the Florida Keys? Why do they call it Key West?

Sincerely
Steven ———

R.S.V.P.
P.S. I hope you come to N.Y. in March.

My dear Steven:

One feels more free of anxiety and worry by being a former rather than actual President—that is if one worked instead of played when President.

My hobby is work—just plain work on things I know something about.

The name Key West *comes from the Spanish word* Cay, *which means an island, and Key West is the most western of the Keys.*

I was not in New York in March as I was working, but I may tell you that I took a day off once in a while to fish among the Florida Keys.

P.S. My birthday is August 10th.

CHEERFUL PEOPLE

Dear Sir:

Could you please send me some information on things like who was in your cabinet when you were president, also could you please send me an autographed photograph of *you* and *your* family. Thank you.

Sincerely,
Ricky ———

Dear Ricky:

I was glad to have your note and your *photograph. I am putting them in the Cheerful People file.*

As to your questions, they require a book, and you can find one in the college library in your town. I lived near there once, and know it is a town made of good people and a good college.

SALARY

Dear Mr. Hoover:

Daddy told me that while you were President, you didn't accept any money, but returned it to the treasury. Is this true? I know you payed all your own traveling expenses in Europe while you were aiding them. It must take a great deal of love of country to do this.

If you run for President again, I would vote for you.

Very sincerely,
Sara ———

Dear Sara:

As to the Presidential salary, I drew it as the law provides. However, I spent it on charity and other public services.

HARDEST JOB

Dear Mr. Hoover:

I am in the eighth grade and am writing a term-paper on the Executive Branch of the United States Government. I would very much like to have your views and opinions on the following questions:

1. What part of the President's job would you consider the hardest? Why?

2. In what ways, if any, do you feel that the President's responsibilities are being added on to his already heavy load?

I would very much appreciate your reply

       Thank-you
        Very Much!!

            Yours Truly,
            Susan ———

My dear Susan:

You ask: "What part of the President's job would you consider the hardest?"

The answer is: *Making a dozen decisions a day.*

You also ask: "In what ways, if any, do you feel that the President's responsibilities are being added on to his already heavy load?"

The answer is: *The Communists add to his burdens every minute of the twenty-four hours.*

PART *3*

On Boys' Clubs and Such

THE BOYS' CLUB

Dear Mr. Hoover:

I am a member of the Boys' Club of America. I would like to know how you started the Boys' Club. I enjoy the Boys' Club very much, and if it wasn't for you there wouldn't be any clubs for the boys' of America.

Well I am sorry but I must do my work for school.

Sincerely yours,
Norman ———

My dear Norman:

I am indeed glad to hear from a member of the Boys' Clubs.

That organization was started over one hundred years ago. I have been the Chairman of the National Board of Directors for the past twenty-five years. It has grown immensely in that time through the devotion of many men and women. Today, you are an association of some six hundred thousand boys.

With good wishes.

SCOUTING

Dear Mr. Hoover:

I have heard that you were a mining engineer before you became president. I have read your biography and I found it very interesting. I have heard of some of the boy's clubs you opened. I belong to the Cub Scouts of America. I am 9 years old in fourth grade.

Sincerely yours,
Jonathan ———

Dear Jonathan:

I deem it a great compliment that you approve of my biography.

I am interested in Boy Scouts as well as the Boys' Clubs. Stick to the Scouts for they are a great American institution.

THE JOB FOR SCOUTS

Dear Mr. Hoover:

We are the Cub Scouts of Den ———. February has been "Presidents Month" for Cub Scouts of America. We have studied Presidents and good citizenship. We would like your opinion on what Cub Scouts can do to be better citizens and serve a country as large as ours.

> Very truly yours,
> ——— Den Chief

Dear Cub Scout Troop:

The job for all Scouts is:
1. Get all the education you can.
2. Cling to your religious faith.
3. You will be a boy or a scout only once. Get all the constructive fun you can.

"PRO DEO ET PATRIA"

Mr. Herbert Hoover:

I am a Sea Scout, 16 years old, and am trying to earn a church award "Pro Deo Et Patria" (For God and country). The requirements for this award are to work in the church for 150 hours, after completing this we are to write a theme or do a project. I am writing a theme, and the title of my theme is What Scouting Means to Me and Others. I know what scouting means to me, but I would like to know what scouting means to others or what others think about it.

Thank you,
William ———

My dear William:

I was most interested in your letter.

There was no Scout organization when I was a young-ster, but I raised a Scout and I have held official positions in the Scouts.

I am all for the Scouts. They build up character, health, and sportsmanship.

So keep it up.

COOKERY CRUISE

My Dear Mr. Hoover:

I am a member of one of our country's great boy's and girls' organizations, 4-H. Through 4-H I have had the privilege of taking many very educational projects. One of these projects is called "Cookery Cruise Around the World." To complete this project, 4-H'ers in our club are required to prepare a report on the culinary customs of countries around the world.

I feel that it is essential that our United States should be a part of my report. I would be honored if you would send me one of your favorite recipes to include in the White House section. This would be a highlight of my book.

I have the honor to remain,
yours faithfully,
Darlene ———

Dear Darlene:

You belong to a wonderful association.
I am sorry I cannot furnish you with a recipe.
I don't cook!
However, I do send you my very best wishes for success in your project.

HOW DO YOU FEEL?

Dear Mr. Hoover:

I am a Cub Scout and we are studying Presidents. I wanted to write to you. Grandmother still talks about you. How do you feel? Did you like being President? Will you be busy? If not, will you send an answer?

> Sincerely,
> Stephen ———

My dear Stephen:

I have your kind letter.
1. I am glad you are thinking about Presidents when a Cub Scout.
2. I feel pretty good at eighty-seven years plus.
3. Being President during great unemployment and suffering from the world-wide depression is not particularly a joy.

I will always be busy, but not too much so not to answer your letter.

CANDIDATE

Dear Mr. Hoover:

Even though I am only in High School I have admired you for a long time. It is wonderful the work you are doing for the Boys Clubs.

Who would you like to see run for President in 1964?

Yours always,
Peter ———

P.S. I am the Chairman of the teen-age Republican Club.

My dear Peter:

I am glad you like the Boys' Clubs. Those clubs now have over six hundred thousand boys from the slum areas who are being given a chance in life—by better brains, character, and physical condition.

As to the Republican candidates in 1964, the only certain thing is that I will not be one of them. Whoever he is, he will need the support of your Club.

COLLECTOR

Dear President Hoover:

I am a Cub Scout. and I am 8-½.
I am collecting autographs for my Wolf badge.
I think you were a very nice president.
Could I have your autograph?

Yours Truly,
Billy ———

P.S. Save this, I might write again.

My dear Billy:

I am glad to be of help toward that Wolf badge. I raised a Cub Scout who turned out to be a great man.

I appreciate your recommendation, "Save this, I might write again."

PART 4

On This and That

AUTOGRAPHS I

Dear Sir:

My hobby is writing letters to famous Americans and asking them to send me their autograph in the form of a letter. I would appreciate it very much if you would be kind enough to let me add your name to my collection of famous Americans.

Thirty years ago my dad wrote to you asking for a similar request. Your answer is one of his most treasured possessions.

Sincerely yours,
Robert ——

My dear Robert:

It is surely desirable that I keep up autograph letters to Robert No. 2—now thirty years after the first one.

AUTOGRAPHS II

Dear Mr. Hoover:

We are starting a collection of autographs. If you could possibly spare the time, would you please send us your real signature. We would prefer this to a photostatic copy. Our collection of autographs is just a hobby.

Gratefully yours,
Bonnie ———

My dear Bonnie:

I can understand your preference for genuine autographs rather than photostats. This is genuine.

I was delighted to see that you are not a professional autograph hunter. Once upon a time one of those asked me for three autographs. I inquired why. He said, "It takes two of yours to get one of Babe Ruth's."

FAVORITE SPORTS

Dear Mr. Hoover:

In 1960 I remember you at Yankee Stadium. I moved from New York on November 14, 1961.

Which are your favorite: baseball, football, and basketball teams? Mine is (in order) Yankees, Giants, and Knicks.

Yours truly,
Frank ———

My dear Frank:

I like football. I once managed a team. I had played sand-lot baseball before I went to college. After I had played a game or two on the freshman team, the Captain said I would make a better manager than a shortstop—so I managed the team. They won most of the games.

GOLF

Dear President Hoover:

I am very much interested in the golfing activities of our presidents. I would appreciate it if you could tell me if you played any golf during your stay at the White House.

Sincerely yours,
Marc ———

My dear Marc:

I have never played golf. While in the White House I played medicine ball before breakfast. It used much less of my working time than golf, and is good exercise.

FISHING

Dear Mr. Hoover:

I am ten years old.
The paper says you go fishing. I do to. What kind of fish do you get? I prefer cat fish. What bait do you use? I use worms.

Love,
Mary ———

My dear Mary:

I have fished whenever I had a chance for over seventy-seven years. I hope you will also. It is good for you. When I was your age I lived in a trout region. I also fished with worms. But a kindly man gave me three artificial flies. I used them successfully until all the wing feathers were worn off.

Nowadays I mostly fish for bonefish with a live shrimp for bait. Bonefish are not good to eat. I put them back in the water so they can grow bigger. Bonefishing around the Florida Keys is especially adapted to elderly gentlemen who can no longer clamber among the rocks and brush. Keep this in mind when you are eighty-seven.

ZOO NEWS

EDITOR'S NOTE: This letter to Betty is of special interest since it is the earliest in the collection. It was written in 1919 when Mr. Hoover was Food Administrator. Unfortunately, the letter *from* Betty has been lost, but Mr. Hoover remembers that she was the daughter of an associate from his early engineering days who was also an associate in the Food Administration. Mr. and Mrs. Hoover gave Tippy, the dog mentioned in the letter, to Betty.

My dear Betty,

I was glad to get your nice letter of August 3rd. I was in London then and it did not catch up with me until I got to Washington.

I am much astonished at Tippy's fighting; it's not proper for small dogs; however, he may reform—they do that generally.

We have in our family

2 small Boys
1 Dog
2 Cats
11 Goldfish
1 Canary
3 Frogs
14 Chickens
2 Turtles
1 Rabbit

And every morning 2 mice. They don't get through the day usually, as Allan needs the traps to catch more and thinks they should be drowned.

We also have 1,000,000 mosquitoes.

PETS AND PRESIDENTS

Dear Mr. Hoover:

I have studied about you a consideral amount of time and I find you are one of my two favorite president. I am in the 6th grade and we have studied presidents a lot.

We have a beautiful house and have a collection of pets. They are a pair of parakeets, a Jacobin pidgeon (a fairly rare bird), a black and brown pair of toy dachunds, a lot of fish, a big black and white striped skunk, and a beautiful cat that is not full grown that weighs over 15 pounds.

You have led an interesting life and I am trying to find out about it.

Please write soon,

Very truly yours,
Jon ———

My dear Jon:

I have your most interesting letter. I was more interested in your liking for pets than in your studying modern Presidents in the sixth grade. I would suggest only Washington, Jefferson, Adams and Lincoln for a study of Presidents at your time of life. Any appraisal of Presidents other than those I mention could well be deferred to your high school or university years.

In the meantime your job is just being a boy with sports and pets and storing in your mind, while in school, the things you may need every day.

DOGS

Honorable Herbert Hover
Walled Off Hotel
New York, N. Y.

Dear Sir:

I read you liked dogs. We have moved into a house with a yard. Mother says I can have a dog. What kind of a dog do you think is the best kind. Where can I get a dog? I have saved two dollars.

Your friend,
Michael ———

Dear Michael:

I like retrievers best for kids. They have an overpowering desire to play ball. And they are good guardians for the home.

However, as your funds are limited, I suggest you write to the Mayor of your town and ask him to give you the first good dog that is sent to the "pound." Most Mayors like to help kids.

CHRISTMAS

Dear Sir:

Our class is writing the important men of our United States to find out what Christmas means to them. Please answer soon.

Truly yours,
Shirley ———

Dear Shirley:

What does Christmas mean to me?
1. We have gone through another year without war.
2. We still have enough left after taxes to buy a Christmas tree and trim it properly.
3. Some of my children, grandchildren, and great-grandchildren will come to see me and the tree.
4. There will be too much to eat.
5. And I wish for all of you in your class a Merry Christmas and a Good New Year.

SPINACH

Editor's Note. This letter, from Mr. Hoover's White House days, solved a real boyhood crisis: Stephen, then aged ten, had lunched at the White House with his father, a long-time associate and friend of Mr. Hoover. Later, when Stephen told his schoolmates about this adventure, no one would believe him, and so he wrote the President for "proof." This letter is the answer. The "button" referred to was one designed for the George Washington Bicentennial of 1932.

THE WHITE HOUSE
     WASHINGTON

                                    February 2, 1933

My dear Stephen:

   This is to certify that you lunched at the White House
with me. I have never been strong for spinach myself, and
I had meant to tell you that you didn't have to eat it.

   In order to make sure that you remember that you
were at the White House, I am sending you herewith a
button which you are entitled to wear as proof thereof.

                         Yours faithfully,
                         Herbert Hoover

HOBBIES

Dear Mr. Hoover:

I not only think you're wise in once being president but in the fact that you still work. It's a proven fact that anyone will live longer if they work.

Along with food, stamp collecting, rocks and minerals are my hobbies. In one corner of my room I have a bulletin board with several pictures of you. I call it "Hoover's corner."

Now as I close I hope it would not be asking too much if you would send me an autograph.

Sincerely yours,
Bill ———

Dear Billy:

I like your observations. I agree that one should not retire from work. If you do you have nothing to talk to your neighbors about except your ills and your pills. They are not interested but want to talk about theirs.

I am also interested in those collections. Making collections is a positive way to keep interested in the world—and I send the autograph herewith.

A TREASURE CHEST

Dear Mr. Hoover:

I am a fifth grader . . . The boys and girls in our class are building a Treasure Chest. We are going to fill it with good manners, right attitudes, and high ideals. Perhaps when you were in fifth grade you started to develop these qualities which made you the successful person you are today. Would you write us a letter stating any facts that are helpful for you. and might be halpful for us in learning these qualities. Thank you for your time and consideration and I hope you keep up the good work.

Sincerely yours,
Kevin ———

My dear Kevin:

I like your idea of a Treasure Chest built into your heart and mind. Once built, it can never be taken away from you.

I did not come by some of these treasures in your way, but through kindly uncles and aunts. Some of their gifts have stuck down to this very day.*

* See "My Own Story," page 147.

DOMESTIC ANIMALS

Dear Sir:

I am 13. When I grow up I want to be a zoologist. Unfortunetly, as of present times I have no domestic animals I have a brother 15, and two sisters 9, and 3.

I have wrote this letter to get your autograph so that I can cherish it the rest of my life. I wish you all possible good health.

Yours Truly,
Henry ———

My dear Henry:

I have your most interesting letter.

I can supply your need for an autograph. But my greater concern is a "domestic animal" for you. Having been a boy once, and having raised two boys, I know this is important.

I suggest you write to the Mayor of your town about it. He must be a good man because I know the people of your town are good people. And they have a surplus of "domestic animals."

A SPECIAL DOG

Dear Mr. Hoover:

I am ten years old. I am in fifth grade.

I have an older brother and sister. I have a pet dog named Duchess. She is part Terrier and part dachund. My mother and father like the idea of having a pet in the house so my mother would have company when she cleans the house.

> Sincerely,
> Debi ———

My dear Debi:

I was greatly interested to hear about that part terrier and part dachshund. That combination surely makes "Duchess" a great pet and a help to mother.

Also, I like mothers and fathers who have girls and boys and are in favor of dogs.

PART 5

On School and Studies

MORE SCHOOL?

Dear Honorable Sir:

Recently at our school a certain question has caused much conversation: "Should the school year be longer for students?" Do you think that the school year should be longer then nine months, or the school day longer then seven hours? I would be very grateful if you could send me your opinion on the question and allow us to publish it in our school newspaper

Most Respectfully,
Randy ———

My dear friend:

The high school and college years are:
1. Too long for those who must work for pay in vacation to help the family or pay their expenses during the school year.
2. Too short for those who wish to speed up their education.
3. All of which varies with the person.
4. You decide.

WHY LEARN LATIN? I

Dear Mr. Hoover:

I am a sophomore in High School. In Latin, I have been assigned the project of writing to prominent people in various vocations to ask their opinion of the importance of Latin.

Since it is a so called "dead" language, should it be discarded from our present day curriculum so that we may concentrate on more practical subjects? Has Latin ever helped you?

I realize you must have a busy schedule, but if you would care to express any thoughts on this subject, I would be very grateful.

Very truly yours,
Rosemarie ———

Dear Rosemarie:

I hope the replies to your inquiry about Latin will be favorable. I am for it. It will open another world to any student, for it creates an interest in the period of the great Roman Empire with its changing form of government, development of literature and expansion of human knowledge. Besides, it is one of the foundations of our language.

WHY LEARN LATIN? II

Dear Mr. Hoover:

For my Latin project I would be very interested in knowing how Latin has been valuable to you during your career, and why high school students should take it. I am fifteen years old and a sophomore in high school.

Very truly yours,
Ann ——

Dear Ann:

Unfortunately I had but a smattering of Latin, and have always regretted that my teacher did not cram it down my throat.

However, that smattering and additional study at that time enabled me to be of some help to Mrs. Hoover in the translation of a great Latin book which had not been put into English. It had been written some four hundred years ago.

The book was a success in engineering circles and copies of it were soon exhausted. Since then it has sold for as high as $250 a copy, but we had none left when that happened.

PUBLIC SPEAKING

Dear Sir:

I am an Iowa boy. I am in the sixth grade. I read that you liked boys and helped with boys clubs. I also read that you helped plan food for many hungry people during war years and that you were a Quaker. I was a Quaker friend first too. But our country church in the timber closed when I was six. We can all drive to another town to a bigger church now. But we miss our Quaker friends.

I had to speak my first piece when I was five years old. Our church was tall inside and had wallpaper and some leaks in the roof. It was Christmas but I saw a fly on the wallpaper. The fly kept bothering me and I couldn't think of my piece.

I read that you answered letters from schoolchildren, so maybe you'll answer mine.

Thank you Mr. Hoover.

Joel ——

Dear Joel:

I also got bewildered in trying to make a speech when I was seven years old in West Branch School. Don't worry, you will make many speeches before you are as old as I am.

SOCIAL STUDIES

Dear Mr. Hoover:

I am in Junior High School. One of the subjects we are taking is Social Studies. We would very much like for you to comment on the value of Social Studies for seventh graders.

We wish to thank you very much.

Sincerely,
Dale ———

My dear Dale:

I do not believe in it at all. What seventh-graders need are the fundamentals of our language, of science, and of mathematics. You can use these every day, and "social studies" should be deferred for a long time—preferably taken when you get to college.

THE ENGLISH LANGUAGE

Dear Sir:

For a display at the school's open house this spring the English IV students are writing a few of the nation's honorable people.

We would like to know how the study of the English language and literature has helped you in your profession. Thank you.

Lynn ———

My dear Lynn:

The answer is, I could not have written intelligently the many reports needed in my profession without some training in English.

You would not be able to get or to hold a good job without it.

GEOGRAPHY

Herbert Hoover
Waldardarl
New York, N.Y.

Dear Mr. Hoover:

In our school when reaching the seventh grade each student must take the class of world gergopahy. I would like to have your opinion on seventh grade world gerogpahy.
Your answer would be very helpful to us.

Sincerely yours,
Charlotte ———

Dear Charlotte:

The study of world geography is important—as is all your schoolwork.

Unless you study and learn about our great country and the world in which we live, you cannot grow up to be a good citizen and an effective person.

Good luck to you.

GOOD BOOKS

Dear Mr. President:

I like very much to read. Some of my favorite classics are "Robinson Crusoe," "Little Women," "Tom Sawyer" and "Huckleberry Finn," "Treasure Island," and "Great Expectations." What were some of your favorite books when you were about my age (12)?

I buy books from a lady who owns a book store that sells really good books, not just "junk."

One day last April, I went out to that book shop to a tea for one of my favorite modern authors, Elizabeth Howard. She showed us her very first draft and the galley proofs for a book she wrote. She told us how she got interested in writing, her sources, how she organizes her books, her problems in finding titles, etc. It was very interesting hearing her.

I hope you have time to answer my letter.

Very sincerely,
Lucy ———

Dear Lucy:

I enjoyed your letter.
You are on the right track in your reading. I am sending
you a little pamphlet which tells about the lady who intro-
*duced me to good books.**

---

* "Thank You, Miss Gray!" by Herbert Hoover, originally published in *The Reader's Digest* is included on page 149 of this
book.

TEXT BOOKS—PLUS

My dear Mr. Hoover:

We are working on a panel discussion for our English class and have chosen as our topic: "What should teenagers be learning in school outside of text book material?"

If you could find time to write to us and give us your opinion on this subject, we would appreciate it very much.

Respectfully yours,
Janet ———

Dear Janet:

1. Being teenagers, remember this period of your life comes only once. It can be the happiest part of your life. Therefore, get all the good fun out of it.

2. Sports make for sportsmanship which, second only to religion, is the greatest moral force in our country.

I wish you good luck and every good thing.

PART **6**

On Choosing a Career

SUCCESS

Dear Mr. Hoover:

What do you think is essential for success?

Respectfully Yours
Richard ———

Dear Richard:

I believe the essentials for success are:
1. *Religious faith and morals.*
2. *Education, including college.*
3. *Do not neglect being just a boy. It only comes once.*

CONVICTION

Dear Mr. Hoover:

I am a young man about to enter college and to launch into life's sea. I do not feel though that I have my course chartered, or that I know where I am going. This is, I know, most presumptous of me, but I would like very much to know how you, with your wide experience, think a life may be successfully used for the benefit of humanity.

Very sincerely,
Timothy ———

Dear Timothy:

I have known many good young men about to enter college who have not, "found themselves"—that is, developed a conviction as to what their professional direction should be.

I have also found that by two years of a broad college course they find themselves. Don't worry. It will come up to you.

DOCTORS

Dear Mr. Hoover:

I was not yet born when you were president. I was born a few days before Eisenhower became president. Although most children my age have ambitions to be president, I have ambitions to be a doctor.

Yours very sincerly,
Kathleen ———

My dear Kathleen:

You were saved a lot of trouble by not being born earlier. I am glad you want to be a doctor and not President. We do not have enough doctors, and there seems to be a sufficient number of candidates for President.

PUBLIC SERVICE

Dear Mr. Hoover:

I am graduating from high school this year and I need advice. I have always been interested in politics and I have seriously thought about it as a profession.

Everyone seems to regard politics as a corrupt, shady profession. I don't believe this is true. How can we say that democracy and liberty are corrupt?

If you were in my position, would you consider politics as a life work? I am an extremely partisan Democrat and will enter the field of politics under that heading.

Thank you very much.

Larry ———

Dear Larry:

I suggest you reorient your mind from the term "politics as a profession" to "public service as a profession."

Politics per se is a transient business and does not lead to a profession. On the other hand, one of the greatest needs of our country is men for public service, and it is a profession of great honor.

There is opportunity in either political party and I wish you well.

ENGINEERING I

Dear Mr. Hoover:

I am in the eighth grade in school, and I want to be a construction engineer. I was told, that before you became a president, you were a great engineer yourself.

Therefore, I have prepared several questions which will help me in making plans for the future. They are as follows:

1. What school subjects and special training are necessary, or helpful, to an engineer?

2. Is English important in this type of work? How? Why or why not?

3. How much English is necessary?

4. How much Math. is necessary?

I will appreciate any information you can give me, and will be looking forward to receiving your letter.

Thank you very much!

Yours truly,
Ralph ————

My dear Ralph:

That was an especially interesting letter to me, and I am glad you wish to be an engineer. Engineers are always working to improve living conditions of people.

As to question No. 1. The foundations of training to be an engineer are the sciences of physics, chemistry and mathematics. But engineers must also have training in geography, government, literature, or they become narrow-minded.

Question 2. English is absolutely necessary as engineers must write intelligent reports and must be able to explain their work or their purposes.

Question No. 3. How much English is necessary? It must include a broad knowledge of literature to make a rounded mind and an appreciable man.

Question No. 4. How much math is necessary? All the elementary mathematics and also algebra, calculus and descriptive geometry. This last one is the test of ability to visualize an engineering project in one's mind before it starts.

CHOICES

Dear Mr. Hoover:

I am 13 years old. I'm getting far enough in school that I have a choose of subject and I've been wondering what I want to be so I can take the right subject next Year.

I have wondered about being an Astronautical engineer, a pilot, or maybe a governor and I've also thought quite a bit about the Presidentcy. I've wondered what it would be like to be the presedent and I thought since you were once the president you could tell what it is like and maybe some of the duties of the president.

Yours truly,
Davy ———

Dear Davy:

I am glad you are thinking of all those occupations—engineering, to be a pilot, a Governor or the President.

The first thing for you to do is to get through high school. By that time your direction may be more clear to you.

In any event, if you want to be an engineer, a Governor or a President, you must go through a university.

It is a good thing for you to think and dream of the future. In the meantime, do not neglect having moral instruction and a good time.

SPACE AGE SPEAKING

Dear Mr. Hoover:

In your years of presidency, I think you did your job well.

It's hard to believe of a man living as long as you.

How did you feel when you became president and when your term ended?

When I grow up I hope to go to Mars. I'm going to try to go to Saturn.

I hope you live many more years.

                    Yours truly,
                    Robert ———

My dear Robert:

You can live as long as I have if you take care of your-self.

I felt sorry when my term in the White House ended, as I believed our program was better for our country than our opponents.'

I am not worried about your ambition to go to either Mars or Saturn. Even at the speed of 17,545 miles per hour made by Colonel Glenn, it would take several hundred years to make that journey. You'd better choose a nearby planet. Two are named for me and you may use them.* However, if you got there you would die as there is no oxygen or water. So, I suggest you stick to the earth for the present.

* EDITOR'S NOTE. In a *This Week* article, Mr. Hoover once told the story of "his" planets, as follows: "At one time two asteroidal planets were named after me by astronomers in Vienna and Brussels. But a world astronomers' association ruled that planets must not be named for living persons and for a time I was without my planets. The association preferred Greek gods. Accordingly, the astronomers who ennobled me thus, took the hint, added classical suffixes to my name and persisted in their purpose. So I still hold the planets—one known as 'Herberta' and the other as 'Hooveria." I was shown one of them through the great telescope at Mount Palomar. Its spectroscope indicated no location for real-estate development."

ENGINEERING II

Dear Mr. Hoover:

I would appreciate it very much if you could advise me as to what high school and college courses to take in preparation for a career in mining engineering.

Sincerely yours,
Jim ———

Dear Jim:

Your question of preparing to be a mining engineer interests me. One of the great engineering colleges of America—the Colorado School of Mines at Golden—is near you. Go there, tell them your ambition, and I am sure they will give you the information you need.

CITIZENSHIP

Dear President Hoover:

Can you please give me your opinions on how we could become better citizens of our country.

Sincerely,
Sharon ———

Dear Sharon:

As you are interested in such a subject, I suspect you are pretty good already. That ladder is not difficult to climb.

1. Hold to and practice your religious faith.

2. Keep going to school until you have finished the university.

3. Take part in the work of your community.

4. Take part in all the legitimate joys with your associates. You will be a girl only once.

I have hopes in you.

WHAT CAN WE DO?

Dear Mr. Hoover:

We have been discussing the many problems which are in the world today. We are writing to you because we are certain that you can give us an answer to the question: "What are some essential things, young Americans like ourselves can do to build a stronger America?"

Yours truly,
Sixth Grade

Dear Children:

It is a good question—and I gladly mention some things you may consider:

The growth of rackets in our cities. The growth of youth delinquency. The increase in crime. The dangers of inflation by increase in wages without equal increases in production. The waste in governments, national, state and local, which increases inflation because of unbalanced budgets. The crisis in our import and export trade whereby we are losing the gold resources behind our currency and credit. The general slump in moral standards with the decrease in religious devotion.

The total of these is a far greater danger to American free men and women than any threat from overseas.

LEADERSHIP

Dear Mr. Hoover:

Recently, in our psychology class, we made a study of today's great leaders in our nation. As a result of the study, you were chosen as one of these. We would like to know what, in your opinion, constitutes a great leader. We want to thank you in advance for your reply to our question.

Respectfully yours,

Mary ———
Secretary of the class

Dear Mary:

Certainly these qualifications include integrity, education, administrative experience, specialized information on foreign and domestic affairs, devotion to the American heritage and the American way of life.

DEFINITION OF DEMOCRACY

Dear Mr. Hoover:

I am in the seventh grade of Junior High School. Recently our Social Studies teacher gave us an assignment, a ten to fifteen page report on what government is. I would like to know if maybe you could write a half page or page essay on your opinions of what government is, since you have had so much experience on the topic.

Respectfully Yours,
Mitchell ———

Dear Mitchell:

I am glad you write me that you are writing a report on government. And you ask my opinions.

That is a most difficult assignment. I am sorry I do not have the time to answer properly.

Perhaps a short definition might be—the organization by representatives of the people of protections for their safety, their freedoms, and their equality of opportunity in life.

SELF-GOVERNMENT

Dear Mr. Hoover:

I am an eighth grade student. In our social studies class we are studying history of the United States and also government.

We have been discussing the self-government of today and at the time of the Northwest Ordinance of 1787. Our history book states: "The Northwest Ordinance provided for three steps which must be taken before the people of the territory could reach complete self-government."

Do you feel that the people of a state have complete self-government? I would appreciate your opinion.

Sincerely,
Charma ———

My dear Charma:

The Constitution of the United States greatly limits this "complete" self-government. To mention only two—the regulation of inter-state commerce and the measures for national defense.

However, the States, desirous of getting into the Federal Treasury, have themselves sacrificed "self-government." Too much self-government has been lost by the States in the last thirty years, and some of it should be given back.

CONSERVATISM

Dear Mr. Hoover:

On our college campus I have been disappointed because I have found very little sympathy to my form of conservatism. Liberalism seems to be the call of the professors. What is your thought on the principles of the true conservative?

Very truly yours,
Gerald ———

Dear Gerald:

There is a lot of fiction and fog around these words "conservative" and "liberal."

My idea of a conservative is one who desires to retain the wisdom and the experience of the past and who is prepared to apply the best of that wisdom and experience to meet the changes which are inevitable in every new generation. The term "liberal" came to the United States in its political sense from England during the nineteenth century. As defined by them at that time, a liberal would be the conservative of today. In 1928, I said:

> "It is a false liberalism that interprets itself into the government operation of commercial business. Every step of bureaucratizing of the business of our country poisons the very roots of liberalism—that is, political equality, free speech, free assembly, free press, and equality of opportunity. It is the road, not to more liberty, but to less liberty. Liberalism should be found, not striving to spread bureaucracy, but striving to set bounds to it."

As you may surmise, in 1962, I believe that the conservative is the true liberal.

COMMUNISM

Dear Mr. Hoover:

I would like to know your opinion on this problem with Russia. How would you try to stop Russia from spreading communism in the little countries? What would you do if someone wanted you to get out of West Berlin? Do you think if we moved all the people out of West Berlin to West Germany that our trouble with Russia over West Berlin would be over?

In case of war with Russia would you suggest that most everybody should have a fall out shelter? We have discussed it in class and had a debate. I would like to know your opinion on this since you have been president and have made several speeches. Thank you.

Sincerely Yours,
Carol ———

Dear Carol:

I am glad you are interested in Communism. Its purpose is to destroy freedom and religious faith, and extend its empire over the whole earth.

The situation in West Berlin involves more than the welfare of a few thousand people. It is a symbol of free people. We must act to prevent this sort of aggression if we hope to stem the red tide over the world.

THE COLD WAR

Sir:

I am a student in Junior High. I would like to ask your opinion on the "cold war". Do you think that communist countries will eventually take over the world? I would also like to know if you approve of bomb shelters. Are they really as good as they seem? Can you give me an idea of what it is going to be like after we get out? Finally the last and most important question. Is there really going to be a war?

I have asked all these questions so that I can know my country better and therefore be a better American.

Sincerely,
Jan ———

My dear Jan:

My opinions are:
1. I do not think that Communism will overwhelm the free world.
2. Opinions on bomb shelters are personal to each person. As for myself, I do not think I would care to be alive when all the birds, animals, trees, houses, and buildings were gone in those places where I had lived.
3. You should learn everything you can about our country. It is the best one on earth.

THE BEST BOMB SHELTER

Dear Sir:

I would deeply appreciate it if you would send to me your views on the need for fall-out shelters. I have had trouble convincing my parents that we need them, and I would deeply appreciate your view.

Thank you!

> Your friend,
> Arthur ——————

My dear Arthur:

Fall-out shelters is a complicated subject.

I assume that if we were to have an attack of nuclear bombs from the Communists, that attack would be directed upon large cities or industrial centers. They would not waste bombs on the smaller cities, towns or villages. Therefore, each locality must be studied for itself as to its dangers.

The best bomb shelter for the American people is a defense establishment that is so strong that the Communists will not dare to attack us. We can be so strong that they will know that the end result of a nuclear war would be that there will be little left in Russia.

JURIES

Dear Sir:

I am a senior in high school. In my English class I am taking part in a debate with the topic—Resolved that the jury system be abolished in the United States. I am very much opposed to this proposition and would like some of your views.

Sincerely,
Al ———

My dear Al:

The jury system has been established in English-speaking countries for about four hundred years. It has proved good in protecting the falsely accused and in sending the guilty to jail.

I have never been tried by a jury and hope never to be. But I am for the jury system.

THREE QUESTIONS

Dear Mr. Hoover:

I am writing in behalf of my 8th grade class. We are conducting a poll of the opinions of some of our nation's outstanding citizens. We would like your opinion on the following:

1. Military censorship
2. Federal aid to education
3. Socialized medicine

Thank you.

Yours truly,
Mary Lou ———

My dear Mary Lou:

I think this is an important poll and I would appreciate it greatly if you would send me the result.

My answers to your questions are:

1. *Military Censorship:* a certain amount is necessary to our defense. Our Army, Navy, and Air Force are maintained as non-political agencies to defend our nation and the whole world. When they try to tell us how to run the government, they are in politics. They should not be censured for telling our men and the country about our common enemy—the Communists. Men who do not believe in our cause will not be good soldiers.

2. *Federal Aid to Education:* I believe the Federal Government should build schools in communities which are too poor to build them. I do not believe in Federal Aid to teachers' salaries. There is no community which cannot pay them if they cut out expenditures on less important matters. If the Federal Government pays them, all my experience shows that eventually it will tell them what to teach.

3. *Socialized Medicine:* I don't believe in Socialism. This country is built on freedom and there is no freedom under Socialism. And besides, the world's experience shows that it leads to dictatorship and loss of the freedom under which our country has grown great and has prospered beyond any nation in the world.

137

CENSORSHIP

Dear Mr. Hoover:

In a recent search through the files of our school library, I ran across a quote made by both you and Mr. Truman on censorship in the libraries. (public)

Would you take a few minutes out of your time and jot down your major viewpoints on the topic of "censorship— restriction of sex in excess from movies, magazines, books, plays, etc."? and send them to me.

Any reply would be more than welcome. Thank you for your time.

Sincerely yours,
Tom ———

My dear Tom:

I have your letter. There are several varieties of necessary censorship. It is necessary to prevent the circulation of obscene literature. And it should be applied to the Communist literature which Soviet Russia sends through our mails.

It is necessary on top defense information.

There is a sort of censorship by our laws supposed to prevent slander, libel and misrepresentation. Unfortunately our courts have steadily minimized the penalties for such action. For example, there is a case of a slanderous book published in both the United States and Great Britain. The American courts gave no damages to the person injured. The British courts gave $25,000 damages.

AID TO EDUCATION

Dear Sir:

I am seventeen years old and belong to the high school debate club. The subject that we are debating this year is "Federal aid to Education." I would be interested in having your position on this subject.

Thank you very much, and best of wishes to you in the years ahead.

Yours truly,
Barry ———

Dear Barry:

I am long since on record in opposition to Federal aid to education for many reasons. Among them—if the Federal Government gets its hands on the schools, they will be in the hands of politicians to get votes and worse, the Federal Government would tell your school what to teach. We have a magnificent public school system managed by the people in the district. Why give that power to Washington?

FOR A BETTER AMERICA

Honorable Sir:

I am fifteen years old and am a sophomore in High School.

Since I admire you and what you have done for our country and the world, may I ask you for your opinion and advice? What can I, as a high school student, do to become a better citizen and an asset to my country?

I wish to express my deepest appreciation for the time and interest which you have given me.

Very respectfully yours,
Mary ———

Dear Mary:

In answer to your questions: to become a better citizen, you must strive to maintain the standards of a Government representative of the people, such as ours. As a high school student, you should study American history and become familiar with our governmental structure. With this knowledge you will be able to understand the ideals and problems of citizenship.

But beyond all this there are two essentials: first, religious beliefs; second, you should get constructive joy out of life, as you grow up.

LAST WORD

My dear Mr. President:

I am a seventh grade student.

Do you have any words of advice for young Americans facing a challenging world?

I wish to thank you for your efforts in our country's behalf.

Very truly yours,
Daniel ———

Dear Daniel:

*I do not know that I have any words of wisdom. But I made a speech at Independence Hall in Philadelphia to high school students, entitled, "The Inheritance of the Next Generation," which I send you.**

---

* See page 155 of this book.

PART 8

"I Enclose . . ."

Included in this part are the following selections, frequently inclosed by Mr. Hoover with his letters to children:

My Own Story

Thank You, Miss Gray!

The Uncommon Man

The Inheritance of the Next Generation

God Bless You

MY OWN STORY

*Prepared in connection with the dedication of the Herbert
Hoover Library at West Branch, Iowa, on August 10, 1962,
Herbert Hoover's 88th birthday.*

Perhaps on this occasion it would not be immodest or in-
appropriate for me to cite my own life as proof that the
doors of opportunity in our country are open to every boy
and girl.

I was taken from this village to the Far West seventy-
eight years ago. My only material assets were two dimes in
my pocket, the suit of clothes I wore, and some extra under-
pinnings provided by loving aunts.

But I carried from here something more precious. I had
a certificate of the fourth or fifth grade of higher learning.

I had a stern grounding of religious faith.

I carried with me recollections of a joyous childhood,
where the winter snows and the growing crops of Iowa
were an especial provision for kids.

And I carried with me the family disciplines of hard
work, that included picking potato bugs at ten cents a
hundred. Incidentally, that money was used for the serious
purpose of buying firecrackers to applaud the Founding
Fathers on each Fourth of July.

The fact that I stand here in this village—a former President of the United States—is proof of what America brings
to her children—and that is a warranty of faith in its future.

As the Quakers say, I can give some "testimony" as to American life. In a long life, as I have said elsewhere, I have seen much of peoples, of governments, of their institutions, and of human woes. I can count up sixty nations with which I had something to do. I was not a tourist. I worked with their peoples. In my professional years I brought to them American technology, with its train of greater productivity and better living. In two wars I served in war-shattered lands, directing relief to the hungry and their reconstruction.

I have worked with great spiritual leaders and with great statesmen. I have lived under governments of free men, Fascists, dictators, and Communists. Their citizens everywhere treasured a confidence that we would maintain freedom and compassion not alone within America, but that we would cooperate to bring it to all mankind.

And what may I say to you as the shadows close around me?

I say to you that today America assures more nearly the dignity of man and the durability of freedom than any other place on earth.

I say to you that America will live because its life is in the hearts of her people, in their religious faith, in their love of freedom and of our country.

May God bring you even more great blessings.

THANK YOU, MISS GRAY!

Reprinted from the July 1959 issue of The Reader's Digest.

I have received a request from *The Reader's Digest* for "the best advice I ever had."

There is another method of changing the shape of things to come than just raw advice for both kids and grownups. And that is the field of tactful suggestion.

At fifteen years of age I left school to practice the profession of office boy in a business firm in Salem, Oregon. One day there came into the office a Miss Gray. She was a tall lady in her thirties, with agreeable manners, kindly eyes and a most engaging smile. I was alone in the reception office. She announced that she was a schoolteacher and asked me about my schooling. I told her I had to work, but I hoped to go to a night school that was soon to open in town. Later I found that Miss Gray's extracurricular occupation was advising—or just being interested in—the young working boys in Salem.

She asked if I was interested in reading books. She must have thought some wider scope in book reading was desirable from my replies to her questions as to what I had read. As a matter of fact, under my austere Quaker upbringing my book reading had been limited to the Bible, the encyclopedia and a few novels which dealt with the sad results of demon rum and the final regeneration of the hero. As office boy, I read only the morning paper, when my superior finished with it.

I also mentioned that outside my office hours I had duties with sandlot baseball and fishing. Notwithstanding this, Miss Gray asked me if I would go with her to the small lending library in town. At the library she said she wished to borrow a copy of *Ivanhoe*, and she gave it to me saying I would find it interesting. I read the book at the office between chores, and in the evenings. It opened a new world filled with the alarms and excursions of battles, the pomp of tournaments, the tragedy of Rebecca's unrequited love, the heroism of the Black Knight and Locksley, and the destiny of Ivanhoe. Suddenly I began to see books as living things and was ready for more of them.

A few days later Miss Gray dropped in again and suggested *David Copperfield*. I can still remember the harshness of Murdstone, the unceasing optimism of Micawber and the wickedness of Uriah Heep. I have met them alive many times in afteryears.

And so, through books, my horizons widened, sometimes with Miss Gray's help, sometimes on my own initiative. I devoured samples of Thackeray and Irving, biographies of Washington, Lincoln and Grant.

At the night school the principal introduced me to textbooks on mathematics, elementary science and Latin. They were important, of course; but, looking back, I realize that the books inspired by Miss Gray also had great importance. While textbooks are necessary to learning, it was those other books which stimulated imagination and a better understanding of life. They made the whole world a home.

They broadened my scope and made me feel a part of the mighty stream of humanity.

At seventeen I went to Stanford University to study engineering. My time was occupied with the required reading and the extracurricular duties of managing the baseball and football teams and earning my way. But occasionally Miss Gray wrote to me and suggested certain books to read.

Miss Gray's influence widened when I began the practice of my profession as an engineer, and it extended over the eighteen years which followed. In that work I had long days of travel, and many hours of waiting for things to happen on ships, railways and canalboats all over the world— from the United States to China, to Burma, to Mexico, to Australia, to Africa, to Canada and to Russia. On one journey, thanks to Miss Gray's inoculation, I armed myself with paperbound volumes of Defoe, Zola and Balzac; on another, with such less exciting books as those of Herbert Spencer, James Mill and Walter Bagehot. Another time I took along Carlyle's *French Revolution,* Gibbon's *The History of the Decline and Fall of the Roman Empire,* and some popular histories of Greece and Egypt. I also read books on Mohammed, Buddha and Confucius, as well as more American history.

With the coming of World War I and with official duties devouring my time and energy thereafter for many years, my book reading slackened. Nonetheless, Miss Gray's influence penetrated even as far as the White House. When I arrived at that residence in 1929 I found it was mostly bare of books except for the published papers of former

Presidents—incomplete at that. One day I mentioned this famine of representative American literature in the White House to John Howell, an old friend and a leading bookseller. Under his leadership and with the co-operation of the American Booksellers Association, some five hundred books were selected. Most of these I had read long ago, but they were much enjoyed by the many other inhabitants of the White House.

To me they were always a reminder of Miss Gray, and of the words of John Milton: "A good book is the precious lifeblood of a master spirit, embalmed and treasured up on purpose to a life beyond life."

I repeat the title of this article—"Thank You, Miss Gray!"; thank you for guiding me to the rich world of wonder, beauty, wisdom and imagination that can be found in books.

THE UNCOMMON MAN

Reprinted from This Week Magazine, *February 6, 1949.*

"The true test of civilization is, not the census, nor the size of cities, nor the crops—no, but the kind of man the country turns out."
—RALPH WALDO EMERSON

In my opinion, there has been too much talk about the Common Man. It has been dinned into us that this is the Century of the Common Man. The idea seems to be that the Common Man has come into his own at last.

Thus we are in danger of developing a cult of the Common Man, which means a cult of mediocrity. But there is at least one hopeful sign: I have never been able to find out who this Common Man is. In fact, most Americans, and especially women, will get mad and fight if you try calling them common.

This is hopeful because it shows that most people are holding fast to an essential fact in American life. We believe in equal opportunity for all, but we know that this includes the opportunity to rise to leadership—in other words, to be uncommon.

Let us remember that the great human advances have not been brought about by mediocre men and women. They were brought about by distinctly uncommon people with vital sparks of leadership. Many of the great leaders were, it is true, of humble origin, but that alone was not their greatness.

153

It is a curious fact that when you get sick you want an uncommon doctor; if your car breaks down you want an uncommonly good mechanic; when we get into war we want dreadfully an uncommon admiral and an uncommon general.

I have never met a father and mother who did not want their children to grow up to be uncommon men and women. May it always be so. For the future of America rests not in mediocrity, but in the constant renewal of leadership in every phase of our national life.

THE INHERITANCE OF THE NEXT GENERATION

*Delivered at Independence Hall, Independence Square,
Philadelphia, June 27, 1961.*

Mr. Mayor:

It is a great honor to receive this distinguished medal
from the City of Philadelphia.

Mr. Mayor, it is with great humility that I speak from
this place so hallowed to every American.

It is a privilege to speak to this great assembly of boys
and girls. Your interest in being in this place, your happy
faces, your bubbling spirits inspire high hopes for the next
generations of Americans. To me, it brings again the thrill
of boyhood.

Too often persons addressing our school students speak
at the level of "Be good and you will be happy." I think you
can take stronger stuff.

Our purpose here today is to pay tribute to those great
men who established a transcendent heritage for the American people. Those men revived the noble concepts of independence of peoples, individual freedom, equality of
opportunity, and the dignity of man.

Mankind, in all recorded history, had seldom before had
the privilege of freedom. And its revival at that time by the
Founding Fathers now sustains a large part of the world.

You will inherit these freedoms and you will have the
sacred duty to maintain them both at home and abroad.

Freedom is a thing of the spirit. But it is not an abstraction. From it comes love of our country. And the spirit of freedom releases the energies and creative impulses of mankind.

Out of this release of creative spirit came the homes, the farms, the factories, magnificent schools, great colleges, huge hospitals, superb libraries, museums, churches, highways, telephones, airplanes, radio and TV. Someday you will inherit them free. They come to you—a gift from the labor and sacrifices of those who have gone before.

Yours will be the job to operate them; and their improvement is never ended, because new scientific discoveries, new inventions, new ideas, new needs will make all of today's physical things out of date in your lifetime. You will need to change and improve them again.

It is difficult to believe how fast change comes upon us from the creative spirit of individual freedom. When I was born—about eighty-seven years ago—there were no electric lights, no telephones, no radio, no TV, no automobiles, no paved roads, no tall buildings, no airplanes, no atomic bombs. There were only small industries; and the railways had only just begun to spread nation-wide.

But do not think that my boyhood was spent in privation. We had warm homes. We had good food. We had good homemade clothes. We had the joys of most of the games you play today.

We inherited those precious gifts of freedom: good schools, good teachers, good universities. We had no fears for the future of our country. And every year on the Fourth of July there were repeated to us the inspiring words of the

Declaration of Independence. From them came a renewed devotion to the great men who met in this Hall one hundred and eighty-five years ago, and a heightened love and faith in America.

Your inheritance of freedom brings you both rights and responsibilities. You have more rights than are spelled out in the Bill of Rights in our Constitution. They have been expanded over the years by law, and by common consent we have interpreted them to include the right of choice.

To retain your inheritance of these rights, you will need not only to know what they are, but to be alert to protest any infraction of them.

Your inheritance of individual freedom cannot be sustained without many restrictions. With changing forces and new scientific discoveries also come new inventions and new methods of evil.

Legislatures devise more and more restrictions. But as to all these restrictions, there is one fundamental test of their wisdom. Do they restrict the creative spirit and the energies which freedom brings? For they are the major impulse of all progress. You should all your life test every legislative act, every social and economic proposal as to whether it unnecessarily limits the energy and the creative spirit.

Today the validity of our beliefs in freedom is at stake on a global battleground. You will need to take part in the struggle.

You will inherit the costly burden of our defense against the implacable foe who lurks in the Kremlin. While we hope for the co-operation of other nations in this defense of mankind, in the end the safety of America must rest upon our own well-armed right arm whatever sacrifice this entails. I am confident of your courage.

What I am saying to you is not a recital of trite banalities, for these rights and responsibilities are the base of our American way of life, and in fact, of our civilization.

Perhaps I may give you a note of confidence from my own inheritance of American freedoms. Our country gave me the opportunity of the public school and a training in my profession at a great university.

In my long life, I have lived and worked in countries of free men, of tyrannies, of Socialists and of Communists. I have seen liberty die and tyranny rise. I have seen slavery again on the march.

Every one of my homecomings was for me a reaffirmation of the glory of America. Each time my soul was washed by relief from the grinding poverty of many nations, by the greater kindliness and frankness which come from acceptance of equality and wide-open opportunity to all who want a chance. I was inspired by the self-respect born alone of free men. There is no place on the whole earth, except here in America, where every boy and girl can have such a chance.

God bless you.

GOD BLESS YOU

Remarks at the
Stanford Commencement, Sunday, June 16, 1957.

President Sterling told me that there was to be a great reform in Stanford Commencement. He said there would be no Commencement Address by some presumed great person. I assumed that he was relieving you of long boredom and a long wait for that piece of paper you have worked so hard to get. Then he promptly asked me to speak to you.

I gave fervent support in his reform on behalf of sixty-two generations of Stanford graduates who have suffered since I was on your spot. No doubt the long Commencement address of my day was full of wisdom and advice. But I do not recollect a word of it—and I doubt if I recollected a word of it ten minutes after delivery.

My mind was—like yours is right this minute—on something else. My total assets were this diploma and $20.22. My thinking was concentrated on what I was going to do next. Besides that, the night before our graduation, my classmates had met and repeated and lustily sang the father song of all modern blues. It was written by the Class Poet and entitled "The Cold, Cold World."

Now in keeping with Dr. Sterling's reform not to keep you waiting, I give you three short observations—but no advice.

Observation No. 1. You are stepping into your second great adventure in life—the first being when you came here. It will be a new adventure every day for the next sixty-two years.

Observation No. 2. You will not find this a cold, cold world. It is full of elders who wish our country to grow in grace and mind. Therefore they wish the new generation every success. They will gladly help if you need it.

Observation No. 3. God Bless You.

Dear President Hoover

I have always been interested in our American history, Especially in our presidents. Your life story was very thrilling, the way you brought yourself up from being a poor orphan to become the President of the United States.

Very truly yours,

Rickey

*T*HIS IS A TYPICAL LETTER *and, at the right Herbert Hoover's original longhand reply, together with the original letter, as finally typed and sent.*